TELL ME ABOUT PIONEERS

MARTIN LUTHER KING

Acknowledgements

Cover (front) Hulton Getty Picture Collection Limited (back) Karsh of Ottawa/Camera Press Limited **Title page** Karsh of Ottawa/Camera Press Limited **page 5** Corbis/Bettmann **page 6** Corbis/Bob Krist **page 7** (top) Corbis/Bettmann (bottom) Topham Picturepoint **page 8** Genevieve Naylor Corbis/Bettmann **page 9** Corbis **page 10** Associated Press/Topham **page 11** Karsh of Ottawa/Camera Press Limited **page 12** Corbis-Bettmann/UPI **page 13** Associated Press Limited **page 14** Corbis-Bettmann/UPI **page 15** Corbis-Bettmann/UPI **page 16** Hulton Getty Picture Collection Limited **page 17** Corbis-Bettmann/UPI **page 18** Hulton Getty Picture Collection Limited **page 19** Associated Press/Topham **page 20** Associated Press/Topham

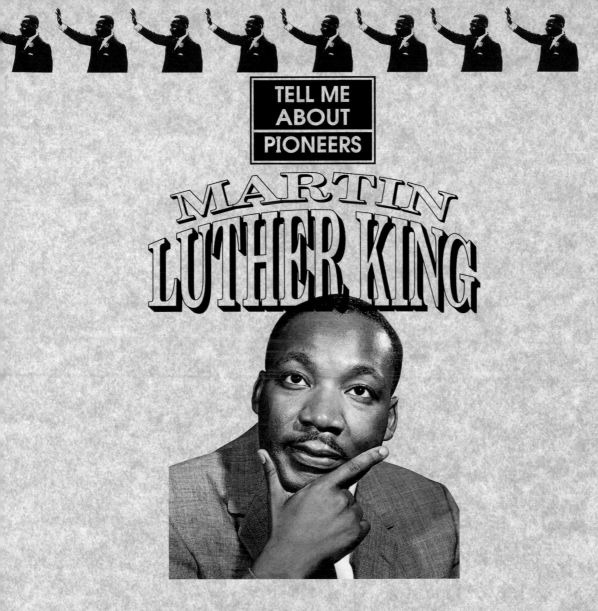

TELL ME
ABOUT
PIONEERS

MARTIN LUTHER KING

written by
John Malam

Evans

Evans Brothers Limited

Contact the Author

Tell me what you think about this book.
Write to me at Evans Brothers.
Or e-mail me at: johnmalam@aol.com

Internet information

Find out more about the civil rights
movement by visiting The National Civil
Rights Museum, housed in the hotel where
Martin Luther King was killed:
http://www.midsouth.rr.com/civilrights/

First published in paperback
in 2005 by Evans Brothers Limited
2A Portman Mansions
Chiltern St London W1U 6NR

© Evans Brothers Limited 1999

First published 1999

Editor: Victoria Brooker
Design: Neil Sayer and Mark Holt
Production: Jenny Mulvanny

Printed in China by WKT Company Limited

British Library Cataloguing in Publication data.

Malam, John
    Tell me about Martin Luther King
    1. King, Martin Luther, 1929-1968 - Juvenile literature
    2. Afro-American civil rights workers - United States -
    Biography - Juvenile literature
    I. Title II. Martin Luther King
    323.1'196'073'092

ISBN 0237528169

In some parts of America, less than fifty years ago, black people were treated very badly by white people. The white people told the black people what they could or could not do. For example, black children were not allowed to mix with white children. On buses, black people could not sit in seats meant for white people.

One man, Martin Luther King, wanted to make things better for all black people in America. He wanted black people to have the same rights as white people. This is his story.

Martin Luther King. He said: "I have a dream that one day ... little black boys and black girls will be able to join hands with little white boys and white girls and walk together as sisters and brothers."

On 15 January 1929, a baby boy was born in a house in Atlanta, a city in the south of America.

At first, the baby was called Michael Luther King, but after a while his parents changed his name to Martin.

Martin lived with his parents, grandparents, brother and sister, uncles and aunts. They lived in a big, old house in a part of Atlanta called Sweet Auburn. Lots of other black families lived in this part of the city, too.

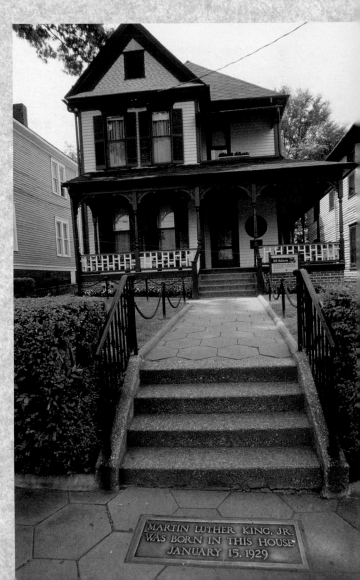

As a boy, Martin lived in this house in Atlanta, in the state of Georgia.

MARTIN LUTHER KING, JR. WAS BORN IN THIS HOUSE JANUARY 15, 1929

Martin's mother was a school teacher. His father was a minister at Ebenezer Baptist Church. It was near the family's home.

Martin grew up in a Christian family. He learned the importance of love and peace, and that God had made all people equal.

▲ Martin's father, who was also called Martin Luther King.

◄ Ebenezer Baptist Church, where Martin's father worked.

When he was very young, Martin had lots of friends. Some were children from white families. Some were from black families.

But when he started school, Martin's white friends went to a school for white children. Martin and his black friends went to a school for black children. Soon, Martin's white friends stopped playing with him and other black children. For the first time, Martin saw how black people were treated differently from white people. It upset him.

At some schools, black children were not allowed to mix with white children. It was called segregation.

When Martin finished school in Atlanta, he went on to study in Boston. Boston is the capital town of Massachusetts, a state in the north of America.

Martin did well at school. He went to college and studied to become a minister, like his father. When Martin was 22, he went to Boston University. It was in the north, hundreds of miles away from his home.

Martin saw that black people in the north of America were treated better than black people in the south. He started wondering how he could help make things better for them.

While he was at Boston University, Martin met Coretta Scott. They had much in common and soon fell in love. They got married in Coretta's home town of Marion, in the state of Alabama. It was a proud day for Martin's father because he was the minister in charge of the wedding service.

Martin and Coretta had four children. Here they are with Yolanda, Martin, and Dexter. Their fourth child, Bernice, had not been born when this photograph was taken.

A year after his wedding, Martin became the minister at a church in Montgomery, Alabama, which is in the south of America.

Martin was busier than ever. He preached at his church, cared for the people in the community, and still found time to finish his studies at faraway Boston University.

In Montgomery, Martin's attention turned to the way in which the city's black people were treated.

Reverend Dr Martin Luther King, aged 26, shortly after he finished his studies at Boston University.

One day, in December 1955, Mrs Rosa Parks, a black woman, was travelling home on a bus in Montgomery. She was sitting in the front part of the bus, which was for white people only. Black people were supposed to sit at the back of the bus.

Mrs Parks was asked to give her seat to a white person. She refused. The police came, and she was arrested.

Rosa Parks, sitting in the whites-only section of a Montgomery bus.

The arrest of Rosa Parks made black people in Montgomery want to find a way of showing how upset and angry they were. They looked for someone who would be their leader and who would speak up for them.

They turned to Martin for help. They knew he was clever, that he was a good speaker, and that he believed black people should be treated just the same as white people.

A protest was organised. Black people stopped travelling on the buses in Montgomery.

Martin and more than 100 black people were arrested during the bus protest. Outside court he promised he would carry on working for all black people in America.

The bus protest lasted for more than a year. Finally, in a court of law, a judge said the bus company was wrong to separate black people from white people. He told the company to stop doing it.

At last, black people could sit wherever they wanted to on the buses in Montgomery.

Martin became a hero for black people all over America. Many white people hated him. One day, someone exploded a bomb at his house. Luckily, no one was hurt.

Once, a cross was burnt outside Martin's house by his enemies.

The bus protest was just the beginning. Shops and restaurants still had separate lunch counters for black people and white people to eat at. Black people protested in towns and cities all over America. Many had food and drink thrown at them.

Martin knew he had to go on working for black people, and to do this he stopped being the minister at his church, in Montgomery.

FOR COLORED ONLY

▲ Black people could not drink from the fountains used by white people.

◀ These black people are protesting at a lunch-counter.

Martin began to tour America. In just eleven years, between 1957 and 1968, he travelled more than six million miles and spoke at more than 2,500 meetings.

He wrote five books and lots of articles for magazines and newspapers. There were many dangers, and once, at a bookshop in New York, he was stabbed and injured.

Not all white people were against Martin. Many agreed with him and went to his meetings.

In Birmingham, a city in the state of Alabama, Martin organised a protest that shocked the world. Thousands of people marched peacefully through the streets. Among them were many school children, singing and dancing.

The police decided to stop the march. They attacked the people with dogs, and firefighters squirted water at them. Martin was arrested and sent to jail.

The march in Birmingham told the world about the bad treatment of black people in the city.

Martin was soon released from jail. He organised more marches. His biggest march of all was when 250,000 people marched in Washington, the capital of America. He spoke to the crowd and gave his most famous speech. This is what part of it said:

"I have a dream that my four little children will one day live in a nation where they will not be judged by the colour of their skin, but by the content of their character. I have a dream today."

Martin and the people who marched in Washington.

Keywords

minister
a person who is the leader of a church

protest
a way of showing that you do not agree with something

rights
the freedom a person has to say or do as she/he wants

Index

segregation
when people of different colours, religions, or beliefs are not allowed to mix with others

speech
a talk given to a crowd

state
the United States of America is divided into fifty parts, called states

In 1964, the year after the march in Washington, the American government made a law which gave equal rights to black people.

In the same year, Martin was awarded the Nobel Peace Prize at a ceremony in Oslo, the capital of Norway. This was the most important award for peace in the world. Martin was the youngest person ever to receive it.

When Martin won the Nobel Peace Prize, he was given a gold medal and $54,000. He did not keep the money for himself. Instead, he gave it to others so they could carry on his work.

Martin's work was not over. In 1968, he went to Memphis, in the state of Tennessee, to lead a march in support of the city's refuse collectors. But while he was standing on the balcony of his hotel, he was shot and killed. America was shocked. The country, and the world, had lost a great leader.

The night before he died, Martin had given another great speech. Here are a few of the words he said:

"I may not get there with you, but I want you to know tonight that we as a people will get to the promised land."

This picture was taken the day before Martin died. He is standing between two friends, on the balcony where he was killed.

Important dates

1929	15 January – Martin Luther King w[ ] in Atlanta, Georgia, USA
1944	Age 15 – he left school and went to Morehouse College, Atlanta
1948	Age 19 – he left Morehouse College, Baptist minister
1951	Age 22 – he began to study at Bost[ ] University
1953	Age 24 – he married Coretta Scott a[ ] settled in Montgomery, Alabama
1954	Age 25 – he became a minister at a [ ] in Montgomery, Alabama
1958	Age 29 – he was stabbed
1959	Age 30 – he left his church
1963	Age 34 – he organised protests in Birmingham, Alabama; during a mar[ ] Washington, he made his famous "I h[ ] dream … " speech
1964	Age 35 – he was awarded the Nobel [ ] Prize
1966	Age 37 – he moved to Chicago, Illinoi[ ] help fight poverty among black people
1968	4 April, age 39 – he was shot dead, in [ ] Memphis, Tennessee